FROM SEA to SHINING SEA

MARYLAND

BARBARA A. SOMERVILL

Consultants

MELISSA N. MATUSEVICH, PH.D.

Curriculum and Instruction Specialist
Blacksburg, Virginia

CHERYL J. EVANS

Librarian
Baltimore County Public Library
Catonsville, Maryland

KATHY MACMILLAN

Library/Media Specialist
Maryland School for the Deaf
Columbia, Maryland

CHILDREN'S PRESS®

A DIVISION OF SCHOLASTIC INC.

New York • Toronto • London • Auckland • Sydney • Mexico City
New Delhi • Hong Kong • Danbury, Connecticut

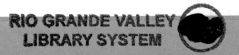

Maryland is a Middle-Atlantic state. It is bordered by Delaware, Pennsylvania, West Virginia, Virginia, and the Atlantic Ocean.

The photograph on the front cover shows the National Aquarium in Baltimore.

Project Editor: Meredith DeSousa
Art Director: Marie O'Neill
Photo Researcher: Marybeth Kavanagh
Design: Robin West, Ox and Company, Inc.
Page 6 map and recipe art: Susan Hunt Yule
All other maps: XNR Productions, Inc.

Library of Congress Cataloging-in-Publication Data

Somervill, Barbara A.
    Maryland / by Barbara A. Somervill.
      p. cm. — (From sea to shining sea)
Includes bibliographical references and index.
    ISBN 0-516-22384-4
    1. Maryland—Juvenile literature. I. Title. II. Series.
    F181.3 .S66 2003
    975.2—dc21   2002001489

TABLE of CONTENTS

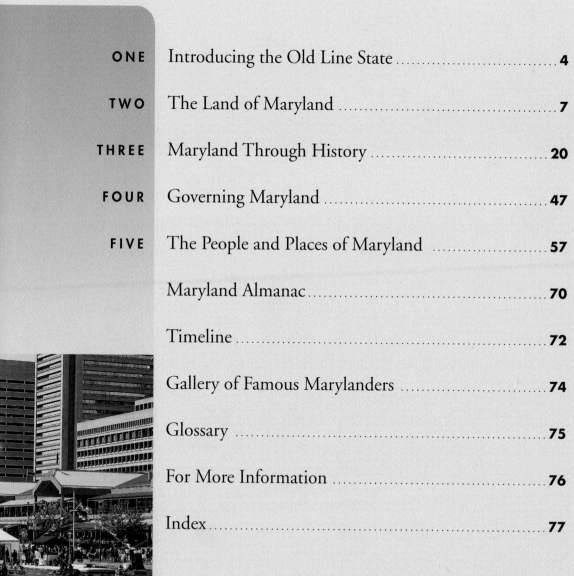

CHAPTER ONE

INTRODUCING THE OLD LINE STATE

A line of seagulls sits on the pier at Belleview, Maryland.

When you think of Maryland, you probably think of crab cakes. Maryland crab cakes are known the world over as a fine dining experience. You might also think about the Chesapeake Bay or Baltimore—two major attractions for Maryland visitors.

Maryland is more than just crab cakes. The state has played an important role in our country's history. Although small in size, Maryland has produced great leaders in our country's government, such as United States Supreme Court Justices Roger Taney and Thurgood Marshall. Others have excelled in the field of medical science, such as Helen Taussig. There have also been many Maryland people throughout history, including Harriet Tubman and Frederick Douglass, who worked to make sure all people are treated equally and fairly.

Maryland was one of the original thirteen colonies. It was named for Queen Henrietta Maria, the wife of England's King Charles I. Maryland's nickname, the Old Line State, came from the days of the Revolutionary War. When Maryland's troops fought against the British, their skill and strength was much admired. General George Washington said that Maryland's "troops of the line" were among the finest soldiers in the Continental army. Because of their efforts to "hold the line" against the enemy, the state came to be called the "Old Line State."

What else comes to mind when you think of Maryland?

- Young cadets proudly marching at the United States Naval Academy
- Children building sand castles at Ocean City
- Fishermen searching for oysters in the Chesapeake Bay
- Fort McHenry, the birthplace of our country's national anthem
- The stone markers of the Mason-Dixon line, the border between Maryland and Pennsylvania
- Canada geese spending winter in the marshlands
- Diamondback terrapins at home along the Chesapeake Bay
- The strange, interesting rock formations of Crystal Grottoes, a cave near Boonesboro

The Old Line State is mountains and shoreline. It is wild ponies and flocks of nesting geese. It is modern Baltimore and historic Annapolis. As you learn more about Maryland, you'll agree that the Old Line State is a fine place to live or visit.

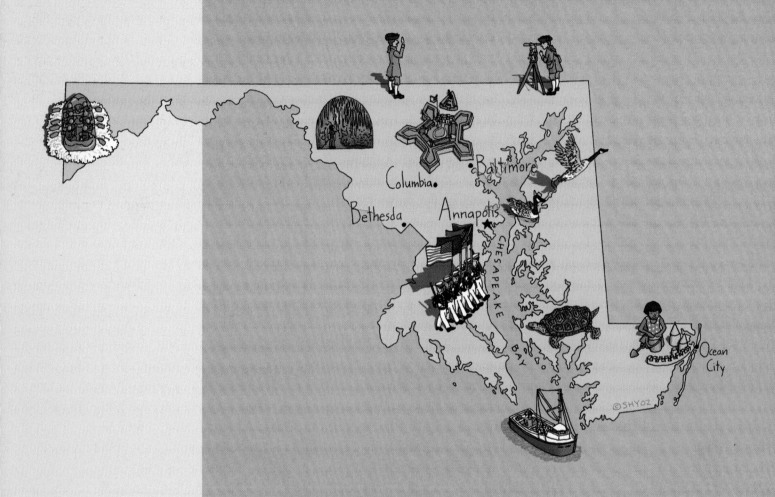

Columbia.

•Baltimore

Bethesda

Annapolis

CHESAPEAKE
BAY

Ocean
City

©SHY02

CHAPTER TWO

THE LAND OF MARYLAND

Maryland is a Middle-Atlantic state, located halfway between North and South along the Atlantic coast. It is sandwiched between Pennsylvania to the north, and Virginia and West Virginia to the south and west. Delaware and the Atlantic Ocean lie to the east. Maryland is oddly shaped, with two land areas that look like lobster claws on the eastern end and a straight northern boundary line. The lobster claws surround the Chesapeake Bay, the state's largest body of water.

Maryland's total area covers 12,193 square miles (31,580 square kilometers). The state ranks forty-second in size compared to the other states. From east to west, Maryland's greatest distance is 199 miles (320 kilometers). From north to south, the greatest distance is 125 miles (201 km). Only three miles (5 km) of Maryland land separate Pennsylvania from West Virginia at the state's narrowest point.

Small boats dot the Western River in Anne Arundel County.

Hikers can get a good view of the Catoctin Mountains from Chimney Rock.

Maryland is divided into three main land regions. They are the Appalachian Mountains, the Piedmont Plateau, and the Atlantic Coastal Plain. Some people also break the Appalachian Mountains region into three smaller divisions: the Appalachian Plateau, the Appalachian Ridge and Valley, and the Blue Ridge.

The Appalachian Mountains

The Appalachian Mountains are the oldest mountains in North America. This major mountain system stretches from Canada to central Alabama, and is made up of several smaller mountain ranges. In Maryland, these smaller ranges include the Allegheny, Catoctin, and Blue Ridge mountains, which run through the state in the west.

The western portion of the state is called the Appalachian Plateau, where Backbone Mountain, Maryland's tallest peak, is found. Backbone Mountain is 3,360 feet (1,024 meters) high. Cities on the plateau include Grantsville, Frostburg, and Swanton.

Between the Alleghenies and the Catoctins lies a broad valley, called the Appalachian Ridge and Valley region. This area is mostly farmland, although small cities such as Cumberland and Sharpsburg are found there. Crops grown in the Appalachian Valley include hay, oats, wheat, and fruit. Many thoroughbred horse farms are also located in this area.

A narrow strip of mountains called the Blue Ridge lies between the Ridge and Valley region and the Piedmont Plateau. The Blue Ridge runs north to south, cutting the state from border to border. Two of Maryland's most scenic state parks—Greenbrier and Washington Monument—are located in the Blue Ridge.

The Piedmont Plateau

The Piedmont Plateau lies east of the Catoctin Mountains. Maryland's piedmont region is made up of flat, raised land. It fills the center of the state. The area has rich soil, rolling hills, and dense forest areas. Farms in the Piedmont grow tobacco, fruit, vegetables, corn, and soybeans. There are also dairy and poultry farms in this region. Many people who live in the Piedmont travel to Washington, D.C., to work. They live in small cities such as Rockville, Wheaton, Gaithersburg, and Silver Spring.

FIND OUT MORE

The term *piedmont* comes from the French words *pied* and *mont*. What do these French words mean? Use a dictionary to find other English words using these French roots.

Maryland farmers raise dairy and beef cattle on the flat land of the Piedmont Plateau.

The Atlantic Coastal Plain

An imaginary line called the fall line divides the Piedmont Plateau and the Atlantic Coastal Plain. The area to the west of the fall line is high and flat. To the east, the land is lower. As rivers flow over the fall line, waterfalls and river rapids are formed. Once boats reach the fall line, they are blocked by the waterfalls and river rapids and cannot go upstream.

Maryland's largest region lies east of the fall line. It is the Atlantic Coastal Plain, and it covers more than half the state. Most Marylanders live on the Atlantic Coastal Plain. The cities of Baltimore, Annapolis, and Towson are all in this region.

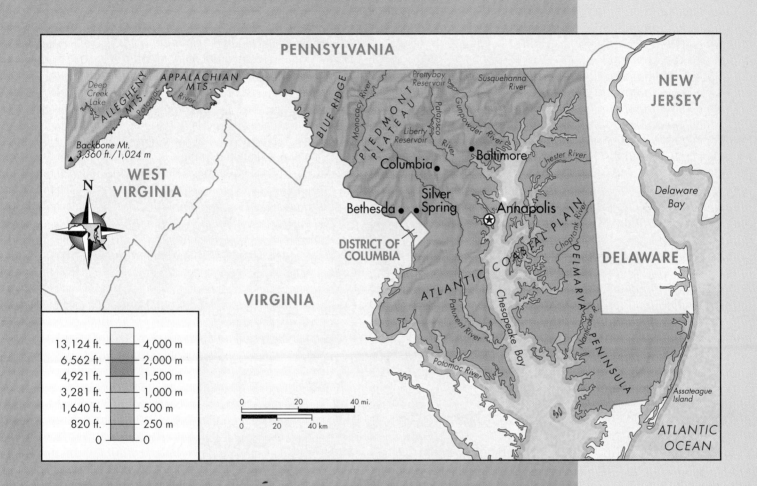

PENNSYLVANIA

Deep
Creek
Lake

APPALACHIAN
MTS.

ALLEGHENY
MTS.

Potomac River

Backbone Mt.
3,360 ft./1,024 m

WEST
VIRGINIA

N

BLUE RIDGE

Monocacy River

PIEDMONT
PLATEAU

Liberty
Reservoir

Prettyboy
Reservoir

Susquehanna
River

Patapsco River

Gunpowder River

Columbia

Baltimore

Chester River

NEW
JERSEY

Silver
Spring

Bethesda

Annapolis

Delaware
Bay

DISTRICT OF
COLUMBIA

DELAWARE

VIRGINIA

ATLANTIC COASTAL PLAIN

Chesapeake Bay

DELMARVA

Choptank River

Nanticoke R.

PENINSULA

Patuxent River

Potomac River

Assateague
Island

ATLANTIC
OCEAN

13,124 ft.	4,000 m
6,562 ft.	2,000 m
4,921 ft.	1,500 m
3,281 ft.	1,000 m
1,640 ft.	500 m
820 ft.	250 m
0	0

0   20   40 mi.

0   20   40 km

Located on the Eastern Shore, the Blackwater National Wildlife Refuge is a protected area of marshlands and forests.

This area is also called the Tidewater because the land is affected by the rise and fall of water, called tides, in the Chesapeake Bay. The Chesapeake Bay is at the center of the Atlantic Coastal Plain. The bay's area is 3,237 square miles (8,384 sq km). More than half of the bay lies within Maryland's borders; the rest is in Virginia.

The Atlantic Coastal Plain is known for having dry, sandy soil, as well as marshy swamps. Farms in this area produce corn, wheat, vegetables, and soybeans. The coastal regions are prime fishing territory, yielding oysters, crabs, and many types of fish.

LAKES, RIVERS, AND A VERY LARGE BAY

When salt water from the ocean meets fresh water from inland rivers, the mix forms an *estuary*. The Chesapeake Bay is a very large estuary. In the bay, water from the Atlantic Ocean meets fresh water from several rivers. The largest of these rivers is the Susquehanna. The Patapsco, Gunpowder, and Patuxent rivers flow into the bay from the

Sailboats pass under the Chesapeake Bay Bridge.

west, while the Choptank, Nanticoke, and Chester rivers flow in from the east.

The bay's shoreline is divided into two parts: the Eastern Shore and the Western Shore. The Eastern Shore is part of the Delmarva Peninsula. The name Delmarva comes from a combination of letters from the words *Del*aware, *Mary*land, and *Virginia*. Each state owns part of the peninsula.

Blue crabs are well-known symbols of the Chesapeake Bay area.

Baltimore and Annapolis are found on the Western Shore. Both the Eastern Shore and Western Shore have active commercial fishing. The fishermen—called watermen—sell their catches to stores and restaurants. The most valued products are crabs and oysters.

The western region of Maryland also has a number of rivers. The Potomac River flows along the Appalachian region's southern edge and forms most of the border between Maryland and both Virginia and West Virginia. The Monocacy River, also in the west, flows into the Potomac.

Western Maryland is dotted with small lakes. Most of these lakes are man-made. The largest is Deep Creek Lake. Other lakes include Liberty Lake and Pretty Boy Reservoir.

PLANTS AND ANIMALS

Two in every five square miles (5 in every 13 sq km) of Maryland are covered by forest. In all, there are more than 150 types of trees found in the state. These include spruce, hemlock, black locust, maple, and oak.

Pines include white, Virginia, pitch, and loblolly. Wild strawberries, blackberries, and raspberries grow in forested areas of western Maryland, as do thickets of wild grapes. The eastern part of the state, which is close to the Atlantic, features many types of grass, sedge, and marsh plants.

Wildflowers sprinkle color on the shoreline and in the woods. Common flowers include Virginia's bower, honeysuckle, and Virginia creeper. Bright yellow black-eyed susans and Maryland golden asters add a touch of sunshine to open fields. Some of Maryland's wildflowers have unusual names, such as hobblebush, black snakeroot, papoose root, wake-robin, and partridge pea.

A wildflower field in the foothills of the Appalachian Mountains comes to life in springtime.

Very few large mammals live in Maryland. Forest and marsh residents include white-tailed deer, Delmarva fox squirrels, red and gray foxes, raccoons, snowshoe hares, rabbits, skunks, and woodchucks. A few bears live in the western mountains.

Reptiles and amphibians are found throughout the state, including turtles, snakes, frogs, toads, and lizards. Snakes common to the state are corn snakes, yellow rat snakes, brown king snakes, striped water snakes, and scarlet snakes.

An interesting Maryland reptile is the diamondback terrapin, which lives along the Eastern Shore. Terrapins are sea turtles that lay their eggs on land. Terrapins were once a food source for local residents. Today, the terrapin is protected by law.

Diamondback terrapins live in salt marshes and tidal waters. They are found on the Atlantic and Gulf coasts from Massachusetts to Mexico.

One of Maryland's most famous animals can be found on Assateague Island National Seashore on the Eastern Shore. The wild ponies on Assateague were likely descended from horses that were brought to the barrier islands in the late seventeenth century. Once a year in July, the ponies swim across the Assateague Channel to the small island of Chincoteague. There they are auctioned off, or sold. The annual pony swim attracts many visitors to the area.

About 250 wild ponies live on Assateague Island, about half of which belong to the state of Maryland.

Because of its extensive marshland, Maryland is a winter home to many migrating water birds, such as Canada geese, ducks, and mute and tundra swans. Peregrine falcons and bald eagles swoop down from the sky above the marshlands to catch fish and rodents. Protected areas for water birds include the Blackwater National Wildlife Refuge and Assateague Island National Seashore.

CLIMATE

Garrett County in western Maryland receives about 83 inches (211 cm) of snow per year.

Maryland enjoys hot summers, crisp fall breezes, and chilly winters. In the Appalachians, temperatures are cooler than along the shore of the Chesapeake Bay. People who live along the shoreline enjoy milder winters, but endure high humidity throughout the year. The highest temperature recorded in Maryland was 109° Fahrenheit (43° Celsius), first recorded in Allegany County on July 3, 1898. The lowest temperature recorded was –40° F (–40° C) in Oakland on January 13, 1912.

Maryland has a high rate of precipitation—rain, hail, sleet, and snow. About 43 inches (109 centimeters) of precipitation falls on Maryland each year. The heaviest rainfall is found along the Chesapeake Bay shoreline and in Garrett County. In Maryland's mountainous region, winter temperatures often drop below freezing. Snowfall is heavier there and averages about 78 inches (198 cm) per year.

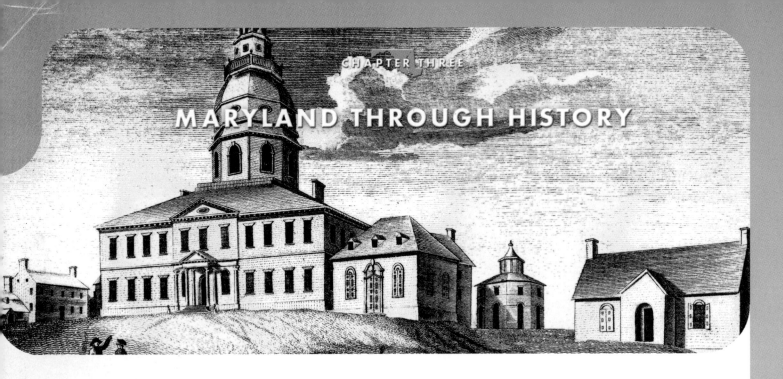

CHAPTER THREE

MARYLAND THROUGH HISTORY

The Maryland State House played an important role in our country's early government.

The first people in Maryland were Paleo-Indians who came more than 10,000 years ago. These people were hunter-gatherers. They hunted mammoth, bison, and caribou and gathered roots, nuts, berries, and fruit. These people did not build villages because they moved often, following large game animals to find food.

Over thousands of years, hunter-gatherer groups learned to farm and build homes. These early people also fished in Chesapeake Bay. By 1500 B.C., small villages dotted the bay's shores. The people gathered and ate oysters. Scientists know this because large mounds of oyster shells have been found near the sites of some of these early villages.

The Adena and Hopewell cultures settled in today's Maryland around 500 B.C. These people were called Mound Builders because they built huge earth hills in shapes of people, birds, snakes, or temples. These cultures thrived for about 1,000 years. No one knows why they disappeared, but by A.D. 1000, the Adena and Hopewell were gone.

Forty small native tribes later lived in the area. Most of these newer tribes spoke Algonquian, a language common to native people of the northeast. The largest of these tribes were the Lenni-Lenape, the Nanticoke, the Piscataway, and the Patuxent. Families lived in small huts made from branches and bark, held together with dried mud. Men hunted, fished, and protected the village from attack by other tribes.

Bear, deer, elk, and wild turkeys were found in large numbers. Fish and crabs were caught in nets from dug-out canoes, while women dug for clams and oysters. The women farmed the land, growing squash, corn, beans, and tobacco. They also gathered wild strawberries and blackberries, nuts, wild root vegetables, and herbs.

Early Native Americans in the Maryland area lived alongside the Chesapeake Bay.

EUROPEANS ARRIVE

Starting in the late 1400s, European explorers John Cabot and Giovanni da Verrazano sailed across the Atlantic Ocean from Europe to what was then called the New World. Both explorers sailed near present-day Maryland but did not set foot on the land. The first European known to actually land in the area was John Smith, a soldier from England who helped set up the first Virginia colony at Jamestown. In 1608, Smith sailed into Chesapeake Bay and explored the land along the shoreline.

However, it was William Claiborne, an English fur trapper and trader, who built the first permanent settlement in the region. In 1631, Claiborne built a trading post on Kent Island, near present-day Annapolis. Claiborne traded food and other goods with local native tribes in exchange for furs. At the time, people in Europe used fur on their clothing to keep warm. Men wore beaver felt hats, and ladies wore trimmed coats, jackets, dresses, hats, and gloves with beaver, otter, and fox fur. Fur-bearing animals were plentiful in Maryland and other parts of the New World, where they were caught and sold in Europe for a profit.

THE MARYLAND COLONY

The year after Claiborne's trading post was built, England's King Charles I granted George Calvert, the first Lord Baltimore, land from the Potomac River north to just above where Philadelphia is today. Calvert wanted to start a colony where colonists could follow their chosen religions. This colony was named *Maryland,* after King Charles's wife Henrietta Maria. Unfortunately, George Calvert died before he could see his new land, and the grant was passed on to Calvert's son Cecilius.

In 1633, Cecilius Calvert's brother, Leonard, and two hundred colonists boarded two ships, the *Ark* and the *Dove,* and sailed from England to Maryland. The ships landed on March 24, 1634, at St. Clement Island. The colonists bought land from local natives and built homes. They soon established the town of St. Mary's. As more colonists arrived,

George Calvert was the founder of the Maryland colony.

the town grew into a city. St. Mary's City served as the center of the colony and its capital for more than sixty years.

The colonial government was run by Leonard Calvert. The Calverts wanted people of all religions to settle in Maryland. Cecilius himself was a Roman Catholic, and he appointed many Catholics to important offices in Maryland. In 1649, the first "toleration" act was passed. Called the Act Concerning Religion, this law provided all Christians the opportunity to follow their own religions.

Both Protestants and Catholics were free to practice their religions in Maryland. Because this freedom didn't exist in Europe at the time, the Maryland colony attracted a large number of settlers. The excellent climate, fertile farmland, and opportunity for success also drew many families.

Maryland's settlers did well in the early colonial days. They cleared land for farms and set up small towns. Crops grown during those early days provided food. Crops included wheat, corn, beans, squash, and tobacco. Soon, Marylanders discovered that tobacco was a cash crop that could make some people rich.

Wealthy settlers purchased land and set up large tobacco farms called plantations. These farms needed many workers. Plantation owners built up a workforce by bringing indentured servants to Maryland. These servants

FIND OUT MORE

A coat of arms tells the history of a family. The Calverts had a very colorful coat of arms that represented both the father's (Calvert) and the mother's (Crossland) sides of the family. The Calvert coat of arms is shown on Maryland's state flag (above). Create a coat of arms to represent your family.

WHO'S WHO IN MARYLAND?

Margaret Brent (1600–1670) was the first woman to own land in her own name in Maryland. She helped run the colonial government after Governor Leonard Calvert died in 1647, even though she was never allowed to vote in the colonial general assembly (the colony's lawmaking body) because she was a woman.

Mathias de Sousa served four years as an indentured servant in Maryland. Later, he traded with Maryland's native people and became an interpreter between Native Americans and the colonists. In 1641, de Sousa was elected to the Maryland Colonial General Assembly. He was the first lawmaker of African descent in the colonies.

Slaves were bought and sold among landowners at slave markets. In some cases, families were separated and sold to different owners.

were actually poor people who wanted to move to the colonies. Landowners bought ship's passage for these people and, in return, the servants worked on the owner's plantation for a number of years to pay for the cost of their trip. Among the first indentured servants in Maryland were three men from Africa: John Price, Francisco Peres, and Mathias de Sousa.

Within twenty years of Maryland's founding, there were not enough indentured servants to keep up with the labor needs of tobacco growers. Plantation owners wanted cheap labor to work their fields. The way to get this labor was to replace indentured servants with slaves. Slavery was a practice in which one person owned another and forced him or her to work. Slaves were brought on huge slave ships from Africa and sold in a market. Once purchased, the slave was owned for life, and if that slave had children, those children were also owned for life. Unlike indentured servants, slaves were not freed after a period of service.

In 1664, Maryland passed a law allowing slavery. Within thirty years, indentured servants were completely replaced with slaves from Africa. Soon, most large plantations were worked using slave labor.

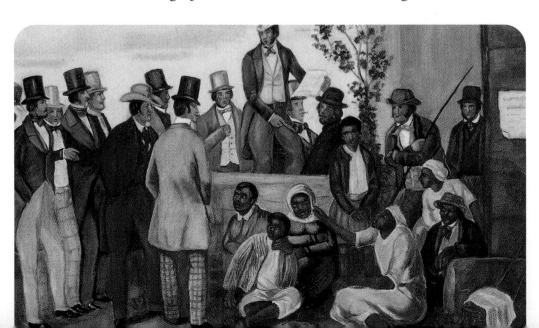

DECLINE OF THE NATIVE AMERICANS

At first, the native tribes of lower Maryland welcomed the European settlers. They sold them land, helped them farm and hunt, and enjoyed friendship with their new neighbors. Unfortunately for the natives, however, Maryland's rich farmland drew thousands of Europeans, forcing native people from their land as small farms, great plantations, and settlers' towns took over.

Not only were Native Americans forced off their land, they also had to fight against the many diseases Europeans brought with them, such as smallpox, measles, and plague. Natives had no ability to resist these diseases. In addition, many tribes fought with each other over hunting rights and land. As a result, many Native Americans died. It wasn't long before there were few native people left in Maryland.

WHAT'S IN A NAME?

The names of many places in Maryland have interesting origins.

Name	Comes From or Means
Maryland	Queen Henrietta Maria, wife of King Charles I of England
Maryland Line	The Maryland side of the Maryland and Pennsylvania border
Chesapeake	Native American word *chesepiook*, meaning "great shellfish bay"
Port Tobacco	Port from which tobacco was shipped to England
Frederick	The son of England's King George II
Rising Sun	A tavern where five wagon trails met

A GROWING COLONY

By the early 1700s, Maryland was an active, profitable colony. St. Mary's City and Anne Arundel Town (Annapolis) had become market centers.

By the mid-1700s, Baltimore was a flourishing tobacco port, mill town, and ship-building center.

The new town of Baltimore was founded in 1729, and became an important port city almost immediately.

Trade between Maryland and England helped build the colony. Tobacco was shipped in huge wooden casks from Maryland's ports across the Atlantic Ocean to London, and the Chesapeake Bay area became known as "the Tobacco Coast." Cloth, tea, glass, and other goods came to the colony on return voyages. In southern Maryland, tobacco became so valuable that it was often used in place of money. In an effort to grow even more crops, plantation owners needed more slaves. About 4,000 African slaves were brought to Maryland between 1695 and 1708—an average of about 300 per year.

WAR AND TAXES

In 1754, the French and Indian War (1754–1763) began between the French and native tribes on one side, and the British and British colonials on the other side. The two sides fought over land and trade rights. Many native people chose to support the French because the French respected the culture and lifestyles of the tribes. The British side included soldiers from England and men who lived in English-run colonies, including Maryland. Colonial men served as scouts or were part of the militia, an informal type of army. The war lasted several years and cost a great deal of money.

In order to pay its war debts, England passed a number of taxes, or extra charges, on certain products sold within the colonies. The Sugar Act (1764) taxed sugar, wine, coffee, indigo, and cloth. The Stamp Act (1765) taxed newspapers, stamps, playing cards, dice, and printed materials. Colonists were furious. They complained of being taxed without having a say in British lawmaking. The colonists called this "taxation without representation."

As a result of the French and Indian War, the British gained control of a large portion of North America.

EXTRA! EXTRA!

In the mid-1700s, the Calverts of Maryland and the Penns of Pennsylvania argued over the borderline between their two colonies. To put an end to the argument, the two colonial governments hired Charles Mason and Jeremiah Dixon to determine the border in 1763. The surveyors placed a stone marker every 5 miles (8 km) along the border. This border, completed in 1767, came to be called the Mason-Dixon line. Even today, it is used as the dividing line between North and South.

Marching through the streets, many colonists protested what they considered to be unfair taxes by the British.

During the next two years, the British passed the Quartering Acts, which forced colonists to house and feed British soldiers in their homes. The Quartering Acts were followed by the Townshend Acts—taxes on glass, lead, paint, paper, and tea. By this time, the colonists were ready to fight back against the British government.

In 1774, the cargo ship *Peggy Stewart* anchored in the Chesapeake Bay. The ship carried tea, which was heavily taxed. An angry mob demanded that the owner set fire to the ship or they would hang him. The ship burned, and the taxed tea sank to the bottom of the harbor.

In 1774, the First Continental Congress met in Philadelphia. The Congress was made up of members from every British colony except

Georgia. Members of the Congress protested against unfair taxes and their lack of representatives to the British government.

The Continental Association was formed that year. This group refused to buy British goods or sell colonial products to the British. Maryland was among the first colonies to join the Continental Association. Colonists who supported the ban on British goods had to do without items such as cloth, tea, glass, and furniture. The ban also cost colonists a good deal of money because the British had once bought most colonial products. The ban had a similar effect on Great Britain. Between 1774 and 1775, British products sold to Virginia and Maryland dropped from over £500,000 per year to just less than £2,000 per year.

On July 4, 1776, members of the Second Continental Congress approved the Declaration of Independence. The Declaration of Independence stated that the colonies were free from British rule. Members from all thirteen colonies signed the document. Charles Carroll, Samuel Chase, William Paca, and Thomas Stone signed for Maryland.

Although the colonies had declared their freedom on paper, this was very different from actually being free. In 1775, the

FIND OUT MORE

Great Britain's money is based on the "pound sterling." The symbol for "pound" is £. Why didn't the colonists measure the loss of business in dollars?

The last of the delegates (representatives) signed the Declaration of Independence on August 2, 1776.

colonies went to war against England to earn their freedom. Maryland's contribution to the American Revolution (1775–1783) included troops, supplies, and privateers (armed private ships). Although the British only invaded Maryland once during the war, the colony's troops fought bravely in the north. Maryland's "troops of the line" were considered among the finest soldiers in the Continental army, the military force that represented the new states. Because of their discipline and military efforts, Maryland came to be called the Old Line State.

While the troops fought on land, privateers fought on the sea. Men who owned ships received a license from the government to seize enemy ships and cargo. During the American Revolution, privateers seized or sank about 600 British ships. Almost 250 privateers were based in Chesapeake Bay.

In 1781, Maryland approved the Articles of Confederation, which was the first step toward the colonies becoming states. The Articles of Confederation was an agreement among the colonies to set up a government separate from the British. The American Revolution ended with the signing of the Treaty of Paris in 1783.

A constitution, or set of rules that runs a government, was written and approved by each new state. On April 28, 1788, Maryland became

Delegates of the original states signed the United States Constitution at the 1787 Constitutional Convention.

the seventh state of the United States of America. Annapolis was chosen to be the state capital.

After the American Revolution, Maryland farm owners expanded their business. Tobacco was still the main crop. Because of the many fine harbors on the Chesapeake Bay, Maryland also built a strong overseas shipping business. Baltimore developed into a major shipping port and soon became the largest city in Maryland.

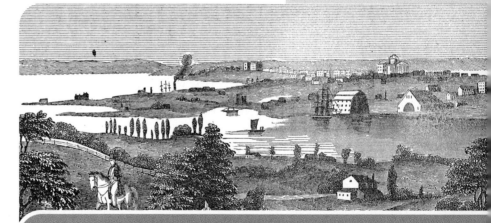

EXTRA! EXTRA!

President George Washington wanted a capital city for the United States that would be separate from any state. He chose the site for the capital on land owned by Virginia and Maryland. Both states gave up part of their land for the new capital, called Washington, District of Columbia (named after Christopher Columbus and George Washington). In 1791, when building began, the site was little more than a swamp. French architect Pierre Charles L'Enfant designed and built much of the city.

Baltimore clipper ships, like the *Corinthian* in this picture, carried valuable cargo between the United States and Europe.

Baltimore shipped goods by fast-sailing vessels called clipper ships. The fast clipper ships built in the Baltimore area were nicknamed "Baltimore Clippers."

THE WAR OF 1812

The peace between the new United States and powerful Great Britain did not last long. In the early 1800s, British ships began stopping ships from Maryland and other states. They seized American sailors and forced them to serve on British ships. The United States protested and once again, war was declared against England.

The War of 1812 was a mix of land and sea battles. In 1813, the British destroyed the town of Havre de Grace, where the Susquehanna River flows into the Chesapeake Bay. Baltimore was another target. However, the city was heavily defended, and the British were pushed back. British troops fired cannonballs and rockets at Fort McHenry in an attack that lasted a full day. The War of 1812 ended soon after the Battle of Fort McHenry.

Marylanders once again turned their attention to ways to earn money. Transportation became a key element in Maryland's growth. By 1818, the first major highway in the United States connected Cumberland, Maryland, in the west with Wheeling, in what was then Virginia. Called the National Road, it provided quicker transportation for products in western Maryland to be delivered to eastern ports.

In the eastern part of the state, a canal—a man-made waterway— linked the Chesapeake Bay and the Delaware River. The Chesapeake and Delaware Canal opened for barges and small ships in 1829. The Chesapeake and Ohio Canal began construction in 1828. The

British ships blockaded the Chesapeake Bay during the War of 1812.

EXTRA! EXTRA!

From a ship in the bay, Francis Scott Key watched the bombing of Fort McHenry. The cannon explosions and the streamers behind the rockets lit up the night sky. This event inspired Key to write "The Star Spangled Banner," our country's national anthem.

The Chesapeake and Ohio Canal brought many new jobs to the Potomac River Valley.

work lasted until 1848, when the canal reached Cumberland. Canals made it easy to ship coal, timber, and other resources from western Maryland to ports in the east.

Railroad travel began around the same time. In 1827, the Baltimore and Ohio Railroad began laying track. In 1830, the B&O Railroad offered the first rail travel from Baltimore to the cities of Cleveland, Cincinnati, and Akron,

FAMOUS FIRSTS

The Baltimore and Ohio Railroad was the first railroad company in the United States; it started in 1827.

The first American umbrella factory opened in Baltimore in 1828.

The first railroad station was built in Baltimore in 1830.

The Baltimore-Union Passenger Railway, the first commercial electric street railway in the United States, opened in Baltimore in 1885.

in Ohio. Steam powered the massive loco-motives. The train reached a speed of 20 miles (32 km) per hour, which was fast for those days. Although shipping products by train was expensive, it was faster than canals. Soon farms and factories shipped all their goods by train.

THE CIVIL WAR

In the mid-1800s, another type of trans-portation system operated in Maryland along back roads and thick forests. Called the Underground Railroad, it was neither underground nor a railroad. It was a secret system of paths and people that helped slaves escape to the northern states or to Canada. Once out of the South, they were free to get jobs and earn money.

In 1860, Abraham Lincoln was elected president of the United States. President Lincoln was against the spread of slavery, which was important to the South's economy. In southern states, most people earned money by farming. Plantations used slave labor to grow cotton or tobacco. In the North, most people earned money

The Baltimore and Ohio Railroad celebrated 100 years of service in 1927.

by working in factories, which employed workers for pay. The southern states feared that Lincoln would try to put an end to slavery. They believed that they should have the right to decide whether they wanted slavery or not. Southerners favored the rights of individual states over a strong United States government.

Before Lincoln was sworn into office, some southern states began to secede, or leave, the Union. They formed the Confederate States of America. In April 1861, Confederate forces fired on Fort Sumter in Charleston, South Carolina. This action was the first battle of the Civil War (1861–1865).

Maryland remained part of the Union, but many Marylanders favored the South. The main crop in Maryland was tobacco, which was grown on plantations worked by slaves. Losing the right to keep slaves would hurt Maryland's wealthiest people. Without slaves, plantation owners would have to pay workers, which would add costs to tobacco and cotton production.

As a result, there were Maryland army regiments in both the Union and Confederate armies. In May 1862, the First Maryland Regiment

(South) fought against the First Maryland Regiment (North) in the Battle of Front Royal. Brother fought brother, father fought son, and neighbor stood against neighbor.

In September 1862, Union General George McClellan sent about 70,000 men to stop General Robert E. Lee's Confederate army at Antietam Creek in Sharpsburg. McClellan's strong forces met Lee's army on September 17. For the next two days, Lee's army retreated across the Potomac into Virginia. Antietam was one of the bloodiest battles of the Civil War. More than 23,000 soldiers were killed or wounded at this battle. The Battle of Antietam was a major victory for the Union army, although both sides suffered heavy losses.

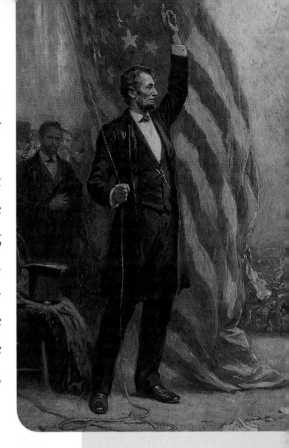

Abraham Lincoln was elected president in 1860, at the height of tensions between North and South.

The Battle of Antietam was the first major Civil War battle on northern soil.

The Civil War ended in 1865 with the surrender of Confederate General Robert E. Lee to Union General Ulysses S. Grant. Maryland's people returned home to rebuild their cities and towns. Although most Civil War damage occurred in the South, Maryland also suffered losses because it stretched along Virginia's northern border. Both armies marched through Maryland and left wreckage behind them. Of the northern states, only Maryland and Pennsylvania suffered significant damage.

The United States was no longer two separate groups, but one reunited country. The job ahead was to rebuild the South, restore train and ship transportation, build factories and schools, and feed the people. This period was called Reconstruction.

BEGINNING OF THE INDUSTRIAL ERA

After the Civil War, plantation life came to an end in Maryland. Slavery ended in Maryland in 1864, when a new state constitution was passed by Maryland's voters. Despite this, agriculture remained strong in the state. Tobacco remained the number-one crop. Dairy and vegetable farms grew. The state also became a center for canning tomatoes and processing seafood.

Baltimore grew as new factories and businesses opened. The city was both a railroad hub and a shipping port. There were plenty of people to work in the factories. The city had chemical, textile, and canning factories. Tomatoes and corn were commonly canned in Baltimore, as were Chesapeake Bay oysters.

Plentiful work brought immigrants to Baltimore from Germany, Ireland, Russia, and Poland. Maryland's population nearly doubled from 267,526 in 1870 to 508,957 in 1900. These immigrants provided cheap factory labor, which, in turn, helped both Baltimore and Maryland to grow.

While factory owners grew rich, workers did not. In 1877, workers for the Baltimore and Ohio Railroad began a labor strike. A strike is a protest and refusal to work. Workers wanted better pay and safer working conditions because many railroad workers were injured on the tracks. One particular danger was getting crushed between railroad cars when hooking one car to another. The strike blossomed into a riot at the Baltimore train depot. Although the riot was stopped, there were hard feelings on the part of both laborers and railroad owners.

Ten years later, the Oyster Wars arose. In 1888, watermen (people who fish on the Chesapeake Bay) from Maryland and Virginia began fighting over fishing territory in Chesapeake Bay. Both sides raided

In the 1870s, Baltimore harbor served as a regional shipping center.

An oyster buyer samples the day's catch on the dock in Baltimore during the 1880s.

each other's oyster beds, and even shot at each other. It took a year to solve the debate. However, once specific territories were set for each state, the Oyster Wars came to an end.

TWENTIETH-CENTURY MARYLAND

The new century began with tragedy in Baltimore. On Sunday, February 7, 1904, Baltimore citizens were stunned when a fire at the John Hurst & Company factory exploded into the worst disaster the city had ever experienced. More than 1,200 firefighters, 57 engines, and volunteers from Washington, D.C., New York, Philadelphia, and Maryland fought the blaze as it spread. By the time the last embers died, 1,526 buildings were destroyed and a seventy-block region of Baltimore was in ashes.

In 1914, World War I (1914–1918) broke out in Europe. At first, the United States chose to stay out of the war, although factories throughout the country manufactured products that supported England and France. In 1917, the United States joined the war against Germany and Austria-Hungary.

A group of women working at the Baltimore and Ohio shops pose for a picture during World War I.

The Aberdeen Proving Ground opened that year in Maryland. It was an army base where bombs, missiles, and ammunition were tested. Maryland's shipyards built war ships for the Navy. Its factories produced canned goods and textiles for the military. In addition, more than 60,000 of the state's men and women served in the military during the war. The war ended in 1918.

For the United States, the war was short and profits were high. Maryland enjoyed a period of wealth and prosperity. However, this period came to a quick end when the New York Stock Market plunged in October 1929. Owning stock shares is the same as owning small pieces of a business. Banks, companies, and individuals bought shares in different companies. When the stock market dropped, the value of the shares also dropped. As a result, stock became worthless, and many

FIND OUT MORE

Many people invest money in the stock market. Look in the business section of the newspaper for the stock report. Choose three stocks from companies that you know, such as Disney or Nike. Record the stock price every day for a week. Did the value of each stock go up or down during the week?

At its peak, more than 600,000 people—including many Marylanders—were employed by the CCC.

people lost all their money. To make things worse, banks had also bought stock using the savings of their customers. They could not give people back the savings that had been lost.

Wages were low in most jobs, and people couldn't afford to buy goods. Companies couldn't sell enough products to stay in business, and many people lost their jobs. This period was called the Great Depression.

More than half the factories in Maryland closed. Thousands of Marylanders lost their jobs, homes, and farms. Baltimore was hit hard by the depression. Long lines formed outside soup kitchens where city residents could get one hot meal a day for free.

To provide people with jobs, the United States government began a program called the New Deal. The Works Progress Administration (WPA) and the Civilian Conservation Corps (CCC) were part of the New Deal. People working for the WPA built roads, bridges, libraries, and other public buildings in Maryland. The CCC fought forest fires in the west and developed national and state parks.

The city of Greenbelt was built as part of the New Deal.

WORLD WAR II

World War II (1939–1945) helped to end the Great Depression. In 1939, the war swept across Europe. The United States did not participate in the early part of World War II. However, the United States sold products, vehicles, and food to France, England, and Russia. Once again, the United States was at work.

On December 7, 1941, Japanese planes bombed a United States naval base in Pearl Harbor, Hawaii. The United States immediately joined the war. World War II was fought in Europe and in the Pacific. Maryland provided ships, chemical products, and food products for the war effort. Thousands of men and women served in the armed forces.

Shipbuilding and aircraft plants in Baltimore were vital to the war. Many people came to the state to work in these industries. Also, a large number of government and military workers moved to Maryland cities near Washington, D.C.

The United States Army tested tanks at Aberdeen Proving Ground during World War II.

POSTWAR CHANGES

Immediately following the war, businesses in Maryland grew. New methods of transportation helped. The Chesapeake Bay Bridge, the Patapsco River Tunnel, and the Baltimore–Washington Airport brought more tourists and businesses to Maryland.

Although most people in the United States lived well during the 1950s, not everyone prospered. Schools and public places were segregated in many states. Segregation means that African-Americans were kept separate from whites. African-American students attended African-American schools, and white students attended white schools.

In many places throughout Maryland, African-Americans were forced by law to use only African-American stores, restaurants, rest rooms, and even water fountains.

In 1954, the United States Supreme Court stated that "separate but equal schools could not, in fact, be equal." They ordered schools to desegregate, or to end the separation. In 1955, Maryland began the process of desegregating its schools.

In the 1950s, Baltimore faced serious problems. The inner city

In 1954, whites protested school desegregation as a group of African-Americans was escorted to class in Baltimore.

was in poor condition. Buildings were falling apart, houses were abandoned, and crime was on the rise. In 1973, the city government came up with an unusual approach to rebuilding its city. Baltimore's government began selling abandoned houses for $1 each. This encouraged people to buy homes in the city, fix them up, and increase the inner city population in a positive way.

Today, other city neighborhoods are being rebuilt, giving Maryland's cities new life. The region surrounding Washington, D.C. has become a major metropolitan area, with many people living in Maryland and traveling to the capital city each day for work.

In recent years, Baltimore has worked hard to encourage people to vacation in the city. The Baltimore Harbor, called Inner Harbor, is surrounded by fun and educational attractions. Harborplace, a 3-acre (1.2-hectare) mall in Baltimore's inner city, offers upscale shopping and dining for both local residents and visitors. The Maryland Science Center and the National Aquarium both opened in Baltimore in the late 1980s.

As Maryland continued to grow, its residents became concerned about the condition of the

Visitors enjoy paddleboats at Inner Harbor, Baltimore's most popular tourist attraction.

Chesapeake Bay. For years, factories and towns had emptied chemical and human waste into the Delaware, Potomac, York, and other rivers that empty into the bay. By the 1980s, pollution had become a serious problem. A joint commission between Maryland and Virginia tackled this pollution problem. The Chesapeake Bay Commission works on planning growth in the bay, preserving bay resources and ecology, and reducing pollution. In 2000, Maryland, Pennsylvania, Virginia, the District of Columbia, and the U.S. Environmental Protection Agency signed an agreement to restore and protect bay resources.

Keeping the bay water clean is important to the state because the fishing industry depends on clean water. The tourist industry also relies on the bay for pleasure fishing, sailing, and beaches. In many ways, the state's wealth and future are centered on preserving the ecology of the bay and its shorelines.

CHAPTER FOUR

GOVERNING MARYLAND

The plan for running Maryland's state government is set up in its constitution. Maryland's first constitution was written in 1776. According to this constitution, people were required to have a certain amount of money or property in order to vote or hold political office. Free African-American men who owned property could vote.

Maryland's current constitution was adopted in 1867. Since then, it has undergone many changes to give Marylanders more rights, such as granting freedom to African-American slaves and allowing women to vote. To amend, or change, Maryland's constitution, three in five members of the legislature must vote in favor of the change. Then the amendment is voted on by the people in the state.

Maryland's constitution divides government responsibilities or jobs into three parts, called branches: the executive, the legislative, and the

The Maryland State House is the center of Maryland's government and a National Historic Landmark.

judicial. No branch is more powerful than another. This balance of power keeps the government running smoothly.

EXECUTIVE BRANCH

The executive branch is responsible for making sure the state's laws are carried out. The governor is the head of the executive branch. He or she serves a four-year term and can be elected to an unlimited number of terms, but may serve only two terms in a row.

The governor has many duties. He or she signs bills (proposed laws), to make a law official. He or she may also veto, or refuse to approve, a law. In the event of an emergency, the governor can call out the state militia (the Maryland National Guard), to help control a situation. The governor also represents the state in meetings with leaders from other states, businesses, or foreign governments.

Governors rely on other members of the executive branch to help run the state. These officials include a lieutenant governor, an attorney general, and a secretary of state. The executive branch has other officials who lead various boards and commissions to handle issues relating to education, transportation, public works, and other things.

LEGISLATIVE BRANCH

The legislature makes state laws. Maryland's legislature is called the General Assembly. Within the General Assembly are two groups: a

MARYLAND GOVERNORS

Name	Term	Name	Term
Thomas Johnson	1777–1779	Thomas Watkins Ligon	1854–1858
Thomas Sim Lee	1779–1782	Thomas Holliday Hicks	1858–1862
William Paca	1782–1785	Augustus W. Bradford	1862–1866
William Smallwood	1785–1788	Thomas Swann	1866–1869
John Eager Howard	1788–1791	Oden Bowie	1869–1872
George Plater	1791–1792	William Pinkney Whyte	1872–1874
Thomas Sim Lee	1792–1794	James Black Groome	1874–1876
John H. Stone	1794–1797	John Lee Carroll	1876–1880
John Henry	1797–1798	William T. Hamilton	1880–1884
Benjamin Ogle	1798–1801	Robert M. McLane	1884–1885
John Francis Mercer	1801–1803	Henry Lloyd	1885–1888
Robert Bowie	1803–1806	Elihu E. Jackson	1888–1892
Robert Wright	1806–1809	Frank Brown	1892–1896
Edward Lloyd	1809–1811	Lloyd Lowndes	1896–1900
Robert Bowie	1811–1812	John Walter Smith	1900–1904
Levin Winder	1812–1816	Edwin Warfield	1904–1908
Charles Ridgely	1816–1819	Austin L. Crothers	1908–1912
Charles Goldsborough	1819	Phillips Lee Goldsborough	1912–1916
Samuel Sprigg	1819–1822	Emerson C. Harrington	1916–1920
Samuel Stevens, Jr.	1822–1826	Albert C. Ritchie	1920–1935
Joseph Kent	1826–1829	Harry W. Nice	1935–1939
Daniel Martin	1829–1830	Herbert R. O'Conor	1939–1947
Thomas King Carroll	1830–1831	William Preston Lane	1947–1951
George Howard	1831–1833	Theodore R. McKeldin	1951–1959
James Thomas	1833–1836	J. Millard Tawes	1959–1967
Thomas W. Veazey	1836–1839	Spiro T. Agnew	1967–1969
William Grason	1839–1842	Marvin Mandel	1969–1977
Francis Thomas	1842–1845	Blair Lee III (acting governor)	1977–1979
Thomas G. Pratt	1845–1848	Harry R. Hughes	1979–1987
Philip Francis Thomas	1848–1851	William D. Schaefer	1987–1995
Enoch Louis Lowe	1851–1854	Parris N. Glendening	1995–

MARYLAND STATE GOVERNMENT

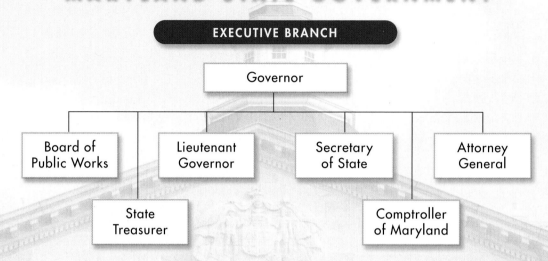

EXECUTIVE BRANCH

Governor

- Board of Public Works
- Lieutenant Governor
- Secretary of State
- Attorney General
- State Treasurer
- Comptroller of Maryland

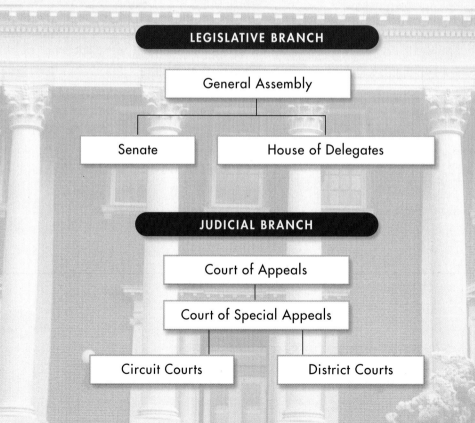

LEGISLATIVE BRANCH

General Assembly

- Senate
- House of Delegates

JUDICIAL BRANCH

Court of Appeals

Court of Special Appeals

- Circuit Courts
- District Courts

house of delegates and a senate. The house has 141 members, called delegates, who serve four-year terms. The state's 47 senators also serve four-year terms.

To create effective laws, senators and delegates serve on different committees. Typical committees include education, housing and welfare, ways and means (taxes and money), and transportation. Com-

Lively discussions take place in this senate chamber when the state legislature meets.

mittees study bills, which are proposed laws. Once a bill is approved by the responsible committee, it must be voted on by the entire General Assembly. Typical state laws might deal with taxes, money for roads and schools, or issues that preserve the environment.

If a bill is passed by the General Assembly, it is sent to the governor for approval. If the governor vetoes (rejects) the bill, the legislature may vote on it again. If three in five members vote in favor of the bill, it will become a law, even without the governor's signature.

JUDICIAL BRANCH

The judicial branch is responsible for making sure all laws follow the state constitution and are fair to the people. It also determines whether someone has broken a law. Maryland's judicial branch has several types of courts to carry out these responsibilities. These include the Court of Appeals, the Court of Special Appeals, circuit courts, and district courts.

The state has twelve district courts and eight circuit courts that handle local trials. Trials for crimes such as murder, robbery, or tax evasion are heard in these courts. The courts also hear cases about traffic accidents and lawsuits concerning large amounts of money.

Decisions from these courts can be appealed. An appeal is a request to have a trial reviewed by a higher court to see if the lower court's decision was fair. Maryland's highest court is the Court of Appeals. Sometimes the Court of Appeals finds that a law is unconstitutional, which means that the law goes against freedoms or rights set in the constitution. The governor appoints the seven judges who serve on the Court of Appeals. However, judges must be approved by the voters before taking office.

TAKE A TOUR OF ANNAPOLIS, THE CAPITAL CITY

Annapolis is a small city of about 35,000 people. It is located on the western shore, about an hour's trip from Baltimore. The city was named the colonial capital in 1695, when it was still called Providence. (The name was later changed to Anne Arundel Town before it became Annapolis.) For a short time, Annapolis also served as the capital of the United States, from 1783 to 1784. It is a city with a long tradition of American history.

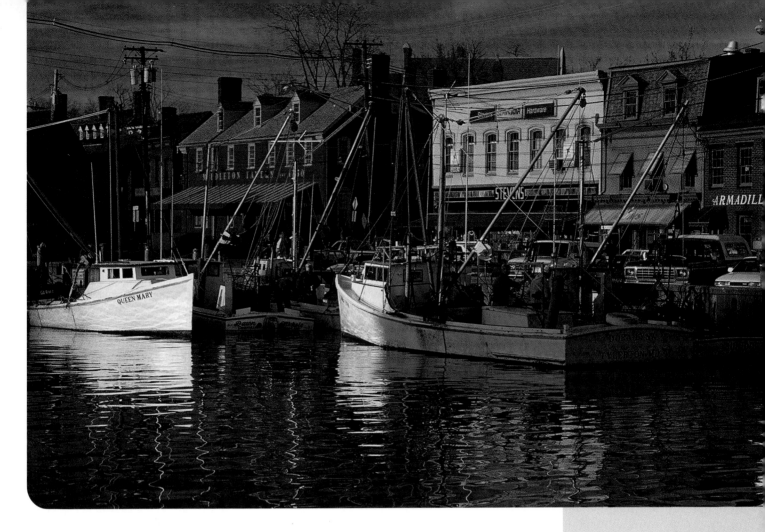

Today, there are more than 1,500 buildings in Annapolis that were built before 1800. A walking tour of Annapolis is like a trip through an outdoor museum. The Annapolis historic district is filled with early wooden-frame homes, brick buildings from the 1700s, and tall, stately Victorian mansions. Registered as a National Historic Landmark in 1965, Annapolis brings colonial times to life.

Begin your tour on the campus of St. John's College. St. John's first opened in 1784, and features many historic buildings and beautiful grounds. During the American Revolution, local citizens met under the

Annapolis is sometimes called "the sailing capital of the United States" because a large number of sailing vessels call the port home.

About 450 students attend classes at St. John's College in Annapolis.

broad branches of a "Liberty Tree" to discuss the war. Although there were Liberty Trees in many colonial cities, the one in Annapolis survived the longest. It was cut down in 1999.

The Maryland State House is the oldest state capitol building still in use. It is the third state house to be built on this site. The first house burned to the ground, while the second was not fancy enough to keep. The main part of the building is made of brick, and it features the largest wooden dome in the United States. There is a lightning rod on top of the building to keep it safe from the many lightning strikes received throughout its 200-plus years. The Old Senate Chamber, where George Washington resigned his office in the Continental army, is open to visitors.

Nearby, Government House is an excellent example of late 1800s architecture. The governor resides at this home, which is furnished with Maryland arts and antiques.

Since 1845, the United States Naval Academy has called Annapolis its home. Although the academy's chief purpose is training naval officers, it also offers an in-depth look at the history of the United States navy. The United States Naval Academy Museum features artwork, uniforms, flags, and displays about the navy. There is an interesting exhibit of handcrafted ship models, which is a must-see for boat lovers. The

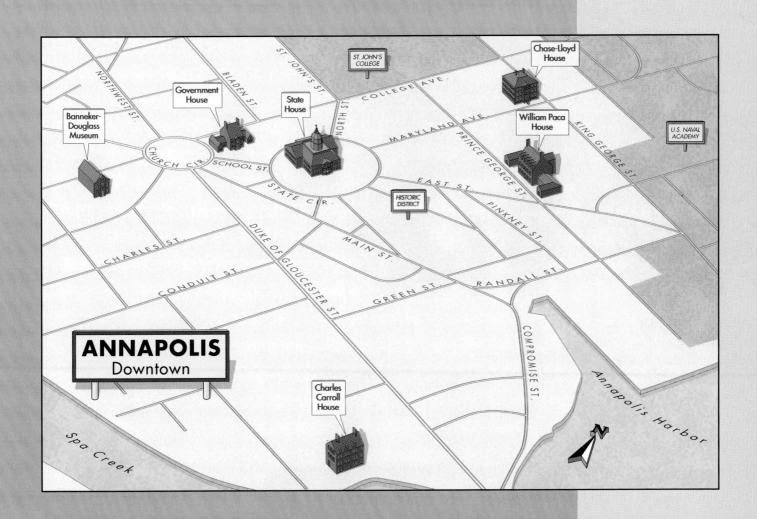

Cadets at the United States Naval Academy participate in a graduation ceremony.

Naval Academy also has a huge cathedral, called the Chapel. The body of John Paul Jones, father of the United States Navy, is buried beneath the Chapel.

After a tour of the academy, be sure to visit the Banneker-Douglass Museum. This museum is named for Benjamin Banneker and Frederick Douglass. It explores African-American history in Maryland and features African-American arts and crafts, lectures, and films.

Next, take a boat tour of the Chesapeake Bay. Tourists can choose among the schooner *Woodwind,* a 48-passenger yacht; the *Annapolitan II;* or the *Harbor Queen.* The double-decker riverboat *Providence* cruises up the Severn River. Considering the naval history of the area, a boat tour is a treat you can't afford to pass up.

Annapolis hosts an art festival every June. The festival features arts, crafts, and music from hundreds of different artists. This event draws thousands of visitors each year.

WHO'S WHO IN MARYLAND?

Frederick Douglass (1817–1895) became one of the greatest American speakers of his time. Born a slave on the eastern shore of Maryland, Douglass escaped to Massachusetts when he was 21 years old. He was active in the Massachusetts Antislavery Society and fought against slavery for many years. He published an abolitionist (antislavery) newspaper, called *The North Star.*

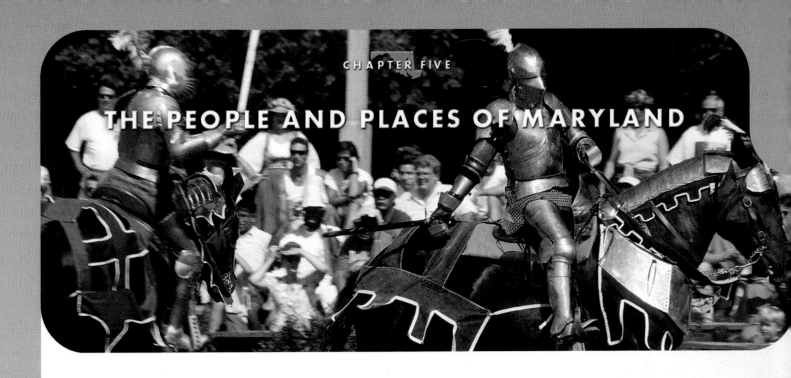

CHAPTER FIVE

THE PEOPLE AND PLACES OF MARYLAND

More than 5 million people live in Maryland. Sixty-four in every 100 Marylanders are of European descent, and 28 in 100 are African-American. Asian Americans make up 4 in every 100 Marylanders. Although this number is still small, it is the state's fastest-growing ethnic group. Asian Americans mainly live in or near Washington, D.C., and Baltimore. Three in every 100 people are Hispanic.

Among those people of European descent, most are German, English, or Irish. People from Poland, Italy, Scotland, and the Netherlands are also represented.

The majority of Marylanders live in the Baltimore or Washington, D.C., area. Baltimore has almost ten times as many residents (651,154) as the next largest city, Silver Spring (76,540). The western region is less populated, with small towns and cities dotting the landscape.

At the Maryland Renaissance Fair, knights participate in jousting, the state sport of Maryland.

Maryland native Edgar Allan Poe wrote frightening stories, such as "The Pit and the Pendulum."

MARYLAND ARTS AND SPORTS

Many Marylanders have greatly contributed to the arts. The state's best-known writer is Edgar Allan Poe, a poet and author of horror stories. Poe's grave is in Westminster Cemetery in Baltimore. Legend has it that on his birthday each year, a mysterious figure skulks out of the darkness to visit the grave. Other writers from the state include best-selling novelist Tom Clancy, mystery writer Dashiell Hammett, Pulitzer Prize-winner Anne Tyler, and children's author Karen Hesse.

The state's musical stars cover a range of styles, from jazz singer Billie Holliday to rock star Frank Zappa. On the classical side, modern composer Philip Glass writes operas, concertos, and symphonies that feature the rhythms and musical styles of Asian cultures.

In sports, the Sultan of Swat and the Ironman of Baseball have both called Maryland home. Homerun hitter George Herman "Babe" Ruth (the Sultan of Swat) hit 714 career home runs and is in the Baseball Hall of Fame. The Ironman is Orioles' shortstop Cal Ripken, Jr., who holds the record for playing 2,632 games in a row.

WORKING IN MARYLAND

Maryland is an interesting mix of factories, farms, mining, and manufacturing. Eighty-two of every 100 workers are employed in service-related jobs. They work as doctors, nurses, teachers, and in restaurants and hotels. Many people also work for the government. Because Maryland is so close to Washington, D.C., many of its citizens work in the capital. Maryland's population continues to grow, creating a higher demand for service businesses and more jobs in the service area.

Although farming and fishing are important to the state's economy, few people work in these jobs. Maryland has only about 6,600 farms. Fifty years ago, there were about 32,000 farms. As with most other states, the overall size of farms has increased, while the number of farms has decreased. Huge numbers of broiler chickens are raised in Maryland, followed by greenhouse items and soybeans. Corn, hay, oats, tomatoes, peaches, and apples are also grown in Maryland. Tobacco is still grown, but most of the crop is shipped to Europe.

Maryland is a major seafood producer and processor. The top market item in this area is crabs, including blue crabs and soft-shell crabs. The Chesapeake Bay provides more than half of all the blue crabs harvested in the United States. Other seafood products include clams, oysters, striped bass, flounder, and perch. Besides fishing, people who work in the seafood industry have jobs in processing, packaging, sales, and marketing.

Across the state, manufacturing is slowly declining. Shipbuilding and steel milling businesses are smaller and hire fewer workers. However, high technology companies are blossoming in Maryland. Hi-tech companies produce computer equipment, software, and support services. Today, the state has more than 6,500 hi-tech companies

Tobacco dries in an enclosed barn before it is sold.

Workers clean and filet fish at Bahia Marina in Ocean City.

If you're looking for another way to enjoy the taste of corn, try this recipe for tasty corn pudding. It will soon become a family favorite! Don't forget to ask an adult for help.

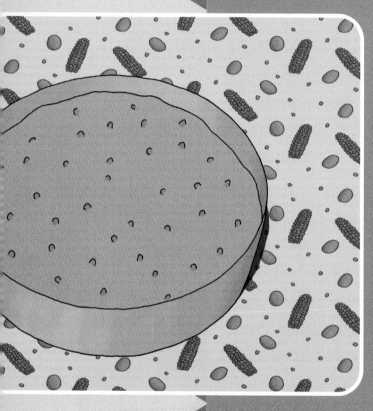

MARYLAND CORN PUDDING

(serves 6 people)
5 eggs
3 cups milk
3 tablespoons melted butter
5 tablespoons sugar
1 teaspoon salt
3 cups fresh or frozen corn

1. Preheat oven to 350° F.
2. Beat eggs.
3. Add remaining ingredients in order, stirring after each addition.
4. Pour mixture into a greased 2-quart casserole.
5. Put 1 inch of hot water in a roasting pan. Place casserole in roasting pan.
6. Bake 1 hour and serve.

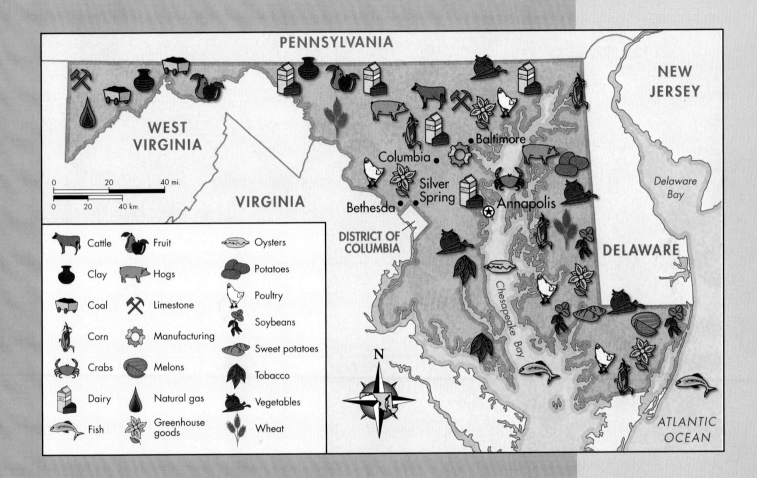

PENNSYLVANIA

NEW JERSEY

WEST VIRGINIA

VIRGINIA

DISTRICT OF COLUMBIA

Bethesda

Silver Spring

Columbia

Baltimore

Annapolis

Chesapeake Bay

Delaware Bay

DELAWARE

ATLANTIC OCEAN

Cattle	Fruit	Oysters	
Clay	Hogs	Potatoes	
Coal	Limestone	Poultry	
Corn	Manufacturing	Soybeans	
Crabs	Melons	Sweet potatoes	
Dairy	Natural gas	Tobacco	
Fish	Greenhouse goods	Vegetables	
		Wheat	

N

0   20   40 mi.
0   20   40 km

doing business throughout the state. Other factories produce items such as electrical equipment and chemicals, or do food processing and printing. The largest companies in Maryland include General Motors, Giant Food, Lockheed Martin, Marriott International, McCormick & Company, and Perdue Farms.

Tourism adds almost $6 billion to the Maryland economy. Tourism is the business of providing food, shelter, and entertainment for visitors. Popular tourist events include the Preakness horse race, Towsontown Spring Festival, Autumn Glory Fest, and the Maryland State Fair in Timonium. Ocean City and other beaches draw thousands of tourists each summer. The wild ponies on Assateague Island are also a favorite with families.

TAKE A TOUR OF MARYLAND

Eastern Maryland

The Atlantic Coast has beautiful sandy beaches, great fishing, and plenty of sunshine. Ocean City is a highlight for tourists, with dozens of great seafood restaurants, amusement parks, waterslides, and miniature golf courses. Water sports are readily available, including deep-sea fishing.

Be sure to take in Assateague Island and its unique wildlife. Early spring and fall are the best times to visit, as the area attracts huge crowds during summer. This national seashore is a wilderness area, remarkable in its natural beauty and clean beaches.

Nearby is Crisfield, the "Seafood Capital of the World," according to local residents. The town is said to be built on oyster shells, although this is mostly an exaggeration. However, oyster lovers will get their fill of these delicacies in Crisfield.

Do you know how to paint a duck? If not, visit the Ward Museum of Wildfowl Art in Salisbury. There you'll find ducks and geese galore: carved wooden ducks, photographs, water paintings, and models. There are many different artists, and each is an expert at creating accurate pictures of waterfowl.

At the entry to Chesapeake Bay is St. Mary's City, a "living museum" that takes you back to colonial days. The Godiah Spray Tobacco Plantation is a real, working plantation with a planter's house, tobacco-drying barns, and slave quarters. Crops are still planted and harvested on this plantation. While in St. Mary's City, be sure to visit the *Maryland Dove*, a replica or copy of a ship that brought early settlers to Maryland shores. The *Dove* features sailing artifacts from the 1600s.

Warm weather, sparkling sand, and a fun boardwalk attract thousands of tourists to Ocean City each year.

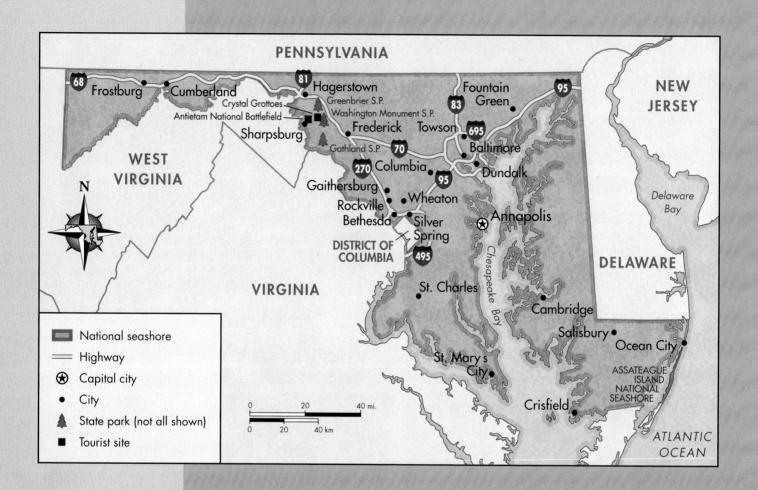

PENNSYLVANIA

NEW JERSEY

68 Frostburg • Cumberland

81 Hagerstown
Greenbrier S.P.
Crystal Grottoes
Washington Monument S.P.
Antietam National Battlefield
Sharpsburg
Frederick
Gathland S.P.
Towson
Fountain Green
83
95
695
Baltimore

WEST VIRGINIA

N

70
270 Columbia
95
Dundalk

Gaithersburg
Rockville
Wheaton
Bethesda
Silver Spring
DISTRICT OF COLUMBIA
495

Annapolis

Chesapeake Bay

Delaware Bay

DELAWARE

VIRGINIA

St. Charles

Cambridge
Salisbury
Ocean City

St. Mary's City

Crisfield

ASSATEAGUE ISLAND NATIONAL SEASHORE

ATLANTIC OCEAN

National seashore
Highway
Capital city
City
State park (not all shown)
Tourist site

0   20   40 mi.
0   20   40 km

The Western Shore

As you head to Baltimore, look for Fort McHenry National Monument. The fort overlooks Baltimore's harbor and was the site of a British attack during the War of 1812. The fort has been rebuilt to its original 1800s condition, and offers videos about the writing of "The Star Spangled Banner."

Fort McHenry is a "star fort," built in the shape of a star with jagged edges. The star design was popular at the time the fort was built.

Plan to spend a day in Druid Hill Park, where you can visit the City Conservatory and the Baltimore Zoo. The Conservatory takes you through the life of a plant. You'll trek through stark desert or bask under leafy tropical palm trees. Christmas and Easter flower displays are particularly beautiful and attract many tourists. The Baltimore Zoo has more than two thousand birds and animals. Watch a rare white rhinoceros share its watering hole with Grevy's zebras. Then, meet the people who earn a living brushing tigers' teeth, feeding hungry penguins, and handling slithering snakes.

For animal encounters, stop by the National Aquarium. Plan an undersea adventure amid more than five hundred tropical fish in the Atlantic Coral Reef. You can handle sea urchins, starfish, and other creatures at the interactive seashore. Among the more interesting exhibits is the world's largest collection of poison-dart frogs. Look, but don't touch!

FIND OUT MORE

Animals belong to different families. Lions and tigers are big cats. Monkeys and apes are primates. Find out which animal families include rhinos, zebras, and snakes.

Visitors watch dolphins perform at the National Aquarium in Baltimore.

All aboard! The country's oldest railroad station is the Baltimore and Ohio depot in Baltimore. Today, the station is a train museum, with samples of many types of railroad cars. The B&O Railroad Museum has everything you ever wanted to know about trains dating back to 1829.

Baltimore is packed with museums. Enjoy the artistry of such famous painters as Matisse, Picasso, and Van Gogh at the Baltimore Museum of Art. At the Maritime Museum at Pier 3 you can check out a World War II submarine, a floating lighthouse, and a Coast Guard cutter at the Maritime Museum. One of Baltimore's most unusual museums is the Dr. Samuel D. Harris National Museum of Dentistry. You will appreciate modern dentistry after viewing George Washington's false teeth and the dental instruments used on England's Queen Victoria!

Central Maryland

Head west to Frederick, Maryland, a town that was occupied by both Yankees and Rebels during the Civil War. Frederick was the birthplace of Francis Scott Key and Barbara Fritchie, who are both buried in the Mount Olivet Cemetery. According to legend, Fritchie waved a Union flag from her house while Confederate troops rode past. True or not, history lovers will want to visit her home.

Two museums worth a look in Frederick are the Children's Museum of Rose Hill Manor and the National Museum of Civil War Medicine. The Children's Museum takes you through a 1790s house and has information about the lifestyles of people who lived in that era. You can visit a working blacksmith shop or see quilts being sewn by hand. At the Museum of Civil War Medicine, exhibits show how doctors coped with sickness and injury in the 1860s.

Legend says that Barbara Fritchie waved a Union flag at Confederate troops as they passed by her home.

A short trip from Frederick takes you to Sharpsburg, site of the Antietam National Battlefield. The battlefield has open rolling hills with a few monuments. A short film provides a historic perspective on the battlefield.

Central Maryland has several state parks and attractions. Greenbrier, Washington Monument, and Gathland state parks offer hiking trails, scenic views, and outdoor sports. The fall color display is spectacular. Washington Monument Park lies along the Appalachian Trail, a hiking

Confederate soldiers hid along the Sunken Road before a surprise attack on the Union Army at Antietam.

trail that extends from Georgia to Maine. Also in this region is Crystal Grottoes, fabulous natural formations created in a series of limestone caverns.

Western Maryland

The rugged region of the Appalachian Plateau offers lots of outdoor fun. You can go white-water rafting on the Potomac or Youghiogheny river. You can also go canoeing, kayaking, trout fishing, and hiking. Deep Creek Lake is Maryland's main ski resort, high in the Appalachians.

Try downhill or cross-country skiing, or head off on a trail in snow-shoes. You'll need to practice so you don't fall into a snowdrift.

Cumberland is a delightful city, once the second largest in Maryland. It still has a turn-of-the-century charm, with Victorian mansions lining the streets and old-fashioned stores in the city's center. Climb aboard the *Mountain Thunder,* a coal-burning train that takes guests on a scenic tour of the region between Cumberland and Frostburg. From the western mountains to the eastern shore, Maryland has plenty of things to entertain you.

View Maryland's fabulous mountain scenery from the *Mountain Thunder* Train.

MARYLAND ALMANAC

Statehood date and number: April 28, 1788; 7th state

State seal: The state seal shows two men holding up the coat of arms. The state motto, *Fatti Maschii Parole Femine,* (Manly deeds, womanly words), is below the coat of arms. The seal is circled with the words *Scuto Bonae Voluntatis Tuae Coronasti Nos,* or "With favor wilt thou compass us as with a shield." Adopted in 1959.

State flag: Maryland's flag contains the family coat of arms of the Calvert and Crossland families. Adopted in 1904.

Geographic center: Prince George's, 4.5 miles (7 km) NW of Davidsonville

Total area/rank: 12,193 square miles (31,580 sq km)/42nd

Coastline: 31 miles (51 km)

Borders: Pennsylvania, West Virginia, Virginia, Delaware, and the Atlantic Ocean

Latitude and longitude: Maryland is located approximately between 37° 53' and 39° 43' N and 75° 04' and 79° 29' W.

Highest/lowest elevation: Backbone Mountain, 3,360 feet (1,024 m)/sea level, along the coast

Hottest/coldest temperature: 109° F (43° C) in Allegany County on July 3, 1898, and at Cumberland and Frederick on July 10, 1936/–40° F (–40° C) at Oakland on January 13, 1912

Land area/rank: 9,844 square miles (25,496 sq km)/42nd

Inland water: 623 square miles (1,614 sq km)

Population/rank: 5,296,486 (2000 census)/19th

Population of major cities:
- **Baltimore:** 651,154
- **Columbia:** 88,254
- **Silver Spring:** 76,540
- **Dundalk:** 62,306
- **Bethesda:** 55,277

Origin of state name: Named for Queen Henrietta Maria, wife of England's King Charles I

State capital: Annapolis

Counties: 23

State government: 47 senators, 141 delegates

Major rivers/lakes: Potomac, Patuxent, Patapsco, Gunpowder, Coptak, Chester, Pocomoke, Naticoke, and Wicomico/Deep Creek Lake, Liberty Lake, Pretty Boy Reservoir

Farm products: Greenhouse products (nursery plants, flowers, seedlings), milk, corn, tobacco, soybeans, peaches, apples

Livestock: Poultry, hogs, dairy cattle

Manufactured products: Food products, electrical equipment, printing, chemicals, computer software, communications equipment

Mining products: Clay, granite, limestone, talc

Fishing products: Crabs, oysters, rockfish, trout, carp, shrimp

Bird: Baltimore oriole

Crustacean: Blue crab

Dinosaur: *Astrodon johnstoni*

Dog: Chesapeake Bay Retriever

Drink: Milk

Fish: Striped bass

Flower: Black-eyed Susan

Folkdance: Square dance

Fossil shell: *Ecphora quadricostata*

Insect: Baltimore checkerspot butterfly

Motto: *Fatti Maschii Parole Femine* (Manly deeds, womanly words)

Nickname: Old Line State

Reptile: Diamondback terrapin

Song: "Maryland, My Maryland"

Sport: Jousting

Tree: White oak

Wildlife: Raccoons, foxes, chipmunks, otters, beavers, white-tailed deer, bears, bobcats, grouses, wild turkeys, partridges, ducks, geese, terns, sandpipers, diamondback terrapins, crabs, shrimp, oysters

TIMELINE

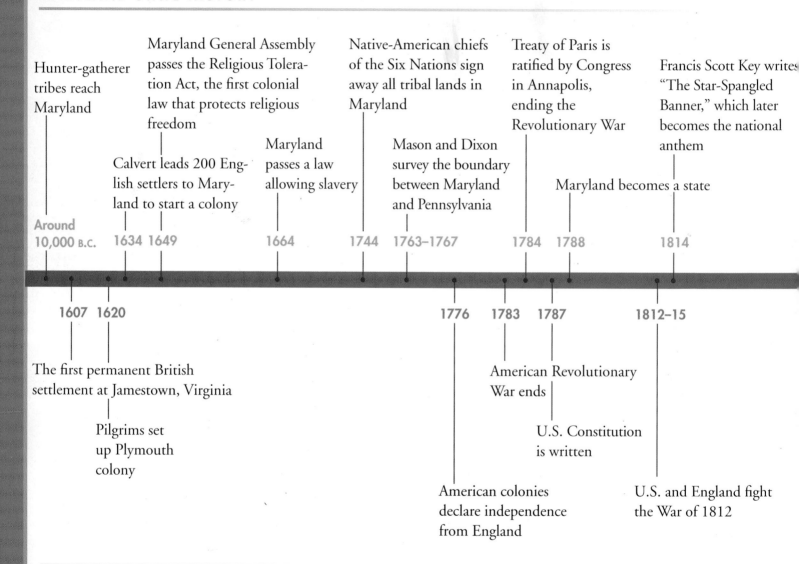

Hunter-gatherer tribes reach Maryland

Maryland General Assembly passes the Religious Toleration Act, the first colonial law that protects religious freedom

Native-American chiefs of the Six Nations sign away all tribal lands in Maryland

Treaty of Paris is ratified by Congress in Annapolis, ending the Revolutionary War

Francis Scott Key writes "The Star-Spangled Banner," which later becomes the national anthem

Calvert leads 200 English settlers to Maryland to start a colony

Maryland passes a law allowing slavery

Mason and Dixon survey the boundary between Maryland and Pennsylvania

Maryland becomes a state

Around 10,000 B.C.   1634 1649   1664   1744   1763–1767   1784 1788   1814

1607 1620   1776   1783 1787   1812–15

The first permanent British settlement at Jamestown, Virginia

Pilgrims set up Plymouth colony

American Revolutionary War ends

U.S. Constitution is written

American colonies declare independence from England

U.S. and England fight the War of 1812

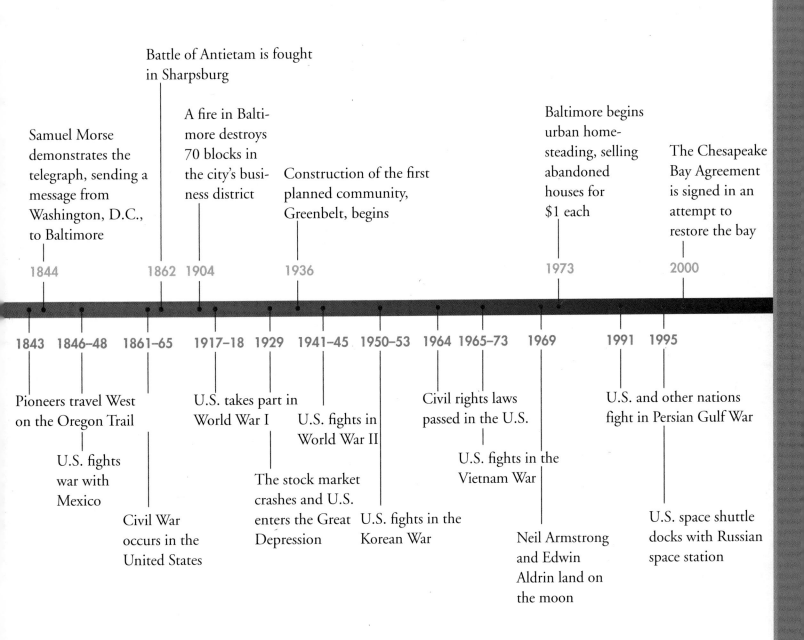

Battle of Antietam is fought
in Sharpsburg

A fire in Balti-
more destroys
70 blocks in
the city's busi-
ness district

Samuel Morse
demonstrates the
telegraph, sending a
message from
Washington, D.C.,
to Baltimore

Construction of the first
planned community,
Greenbelt, begins

Baltimore begins
urban home-
steading, selling
abandoned
houses for
$1 each

The Chesapeake
Bay Agreement
is signed in an
attempt to
restore the bay

1844   1862 1904   1936   1973   2000

1843   1846–48   1861–65   1917–18   1929   1941–45   1950–53   1964 1965–73   1969   1991   1995

Pioneers travel West
on the Oregon Trail

U.S. fights
war with
Mexico

Civil War
occurs in the
United States

U.S. takes part in
World War I

U.S. fights in
World War II

The stock market
crashes and U.S.
enters the Great
Depression

U.S. fights in the
Korean War

Civil rights laws
passed in the U.S.

U.S. fights in the
Vietnam War

Neil Armstrong
and Edwin
Aldrin land on
the moon

U.S. and other nations
fight in Persian Gulf War

U.S. space shuttle
docks with Russian
space station

GALLERY OF FAMOUS MARYLANDERS

Spiro T. Agnew
(1918–1996)
Former Maryland governor and United States vice president (1969–1973). He resigned as Richard Nixon's vice president in 1973. Born in Baltimore.

John S. Barth
(1930–)
Novelist and short-story writer. Winner of the 1973 National Book Award for *Chimera,* a collection of three short novels. Born in Cambridge.

Eubie Blake
(1883–1983)
Ragtime and jazz pianist and composer of several ragtime songs. Born in Baltimore.

Matthew Henson
(1866–1955)
An explorer who was one of the first men to reach the North Pole in 1909. Born in Charles County.

Thurgood Marshall
(1908–1993)
The first African-American to serve on the U.S. Supreme Court. As a lawyer and justice, he worked to guarantee the civil rights of African-Americans. As a lawyer, Marshall won the *Brown v. Board of Education* case by arguing that "separate but equal" education was not really equal and was, therefore, illegal. Born in Baltimore.

Barbara Mikulski
(1936–)
The first woman to hold a statewide office in Maryland. A member of the United States House of Representatives and then the United States Senate. Born in Baltimore.

Cal Ripken, Jr.
(1960–)
Shortstop for the Baltimore Orioles. He holds the record for the most consecutive games played in professional baseball. Born in Havre de Grace.

Roger Brooke Taney
(1777–1864)
Chief Justice of the United States Supreme Court during the 1800s. Formed the leading decision of the Dred Scott case. Born in Calvert County.

Helen Taussig
(1898–1986)
One of the first women to study children's medicine. A pioneer in researching heart problems in babies. Studied and researched at Johns Hopkins University.

GLOSSARY

amendment: change in a law or document

capital: city that is the center of a state or national government

capitol: building in which a government meets

climate: an area's weather conditions over a long period of time

constitution: document that sets out rules and laws that run a government and lists the rights of people ruled by that government

depression: period when business is slow and people have no work or income

ecology: the balance of plant and animal life in a region

economy: how goods and services are produced; how people make money

immigrant: person who leaves one country to move to another country

indentured servant: person who works for another for a period of time to pay a debt

integration: mixing races in public places and facilities

legislature: a group of people who make laws

manufacture: to make large numbers of products by hand or machinery

peninsula: body of land surrounded by water on three sides

plantation: large farm on which one main crop is grown

pollution: harmful materials, such as waste, certain gases, and some chemicals, that make air, water, or soil dirty or unsafe

population: the number and mix of people in a region

prosperity: a period of wealth or success

segregation: keeping races separate in public places and facilities

slavery: system of people owning other people

surveyor: one who measures land and sets borders

tourism: the business of providing hotels, restaurants, and entertainment for visitors

transportation: system of roads, trains, buses, and airports

urban renewal: rebuilding a city

FOR MORE INFORMATION

Web sites

Maryland Kids Room
http://www.mdisfun.org/kids/history.asp
Information about the history, topography, and regions of Maryland.

Maryland State Archives
http://www.mdarchives.state.md.us/
Information about Maryland's history, government, and state symbols.

Maryland Historical Society
http://www.mdhs.org/
Information about the Historical Society's museum and its exhibits.

Maryland Electronic Capital
http://www.mec.state.md.us
Information about Maryland's government.

Books

Burns, Bree. *Harriet Tubman.* Broomall, PA: Chelsea House, 1994.

Jensen, Ann. *Leonard Calvert and the Maryland Adventure.* Centreville, MD: Tidewater Publications, 1998.

Kent, Deborah. *Thurgood Marshall and the Supreme Court.* Danbury, CT: Children's Press, 1997.

Sakurai, Gail. *The Thirteen Colonies.* Danbury, CT: Children's Press, 2000.

Addresses

Governor's Office
Maryland State House
Annapolis, MD 21401

Maryland Office of Travel and Tourism
217 E. Redwood Street, 9th Floor
Baltimore, MD 21202

Maryland Historical Society
201 W. Monument Street
Baltimore, MD 21201

Greater Baltimore Committee
111 S. Calvert Street, Suite 1500
Baltimore, MD 21202-6180

INDEX

ABOUT THE AUTHOR

Barbara Somervill's first visit to Maryland was passing through the state on her way to Florida. Crossing the Chesapeake Bay Tunnel Bridge was an event she remembers well. To find information for this book, Barbara surfed the Internet, called Chambers of Commerce and tourist bureaus, and visited to the local library.

Barbara was raised and educated in New York. She's also lived in Toronto, Canada; Canberra, Australia; California; and South Carolina. She is the mother of four boys and a dog; and she is the proud grandmother of Lilly.